The World's Strangest Forgotten Conspiracy Theories

The World's Strangest Forgotten Conspiracy Theories

Conrad Bauer

Copyrights

All rights reserved © Conrad Bauer and Maplewood Publishing. No part of this publication or the information in it may be quoted from or reproduced in any form by means such as printing, scanning, photocopying, or otherwise without prior written permission of the copyright holder.

Disclaimer and Terms of Use

Effort has been made to ensure that the information in this book is accurate and complete. However, the author and the publisher do not warrant the accuracy of the information, text, and graphics contained within the book due to the rapidly changing nature of science, research, known and unknown facts, and internet. The author and the publisher do not hold any responsibility for errors, omissions, or contrary interpretation of the subject matter herein. This book is presented solely for motivational and informational purposes only

ISBN-13:978-1519491053

Printed in the United States

MAPLEWOOD PUBLISHING

Contents

Introduction 1
Pearl Harbor 3
The Two Babylons Theory 13
The Imposed Death of the Electric Car 23
Garry Kasparov versus Deep Blue 31
Chemtrails 41
Was AIDS constructed as a weapon? 51
The Lost Cosmonauts 61
The Phantom Time Hypothesis 71
The PRISM Network 81
Conclusion 91
Further Reading 93
Excerpt from Conrad Bauer's book The Knights Templar 95
About the author 108
    More Books from Conrad Bauer 109

Introduction

Everyone has that one theory they're absolutely convinced is true. Occasionally, we all stray from the generally accepted facts, and if we're eventually proved right, it's an incredibly satisfying feeling. While these theories typically revolve around the mundane aspects of our day-to-day lives, there is the occasional theory that goes a little deeper. When we move away from the ordinary and towards the powerful, the influential, and the important, these theories begin to take on an additional level of significance. When you suspect that more than one person is involved and is perhaps trying to hide the truth, you've uncovered a conspiracy theory.

But the idea of the conspiracy theory has, in recent years, taken on a negative perception. With many people quick to dismiss these theories as being strange, convoluted, and the product of people with too much time on their hands, they can actually be one of the best ways to peel back the veil of miscomprehension and look closer at the actual facts in any kind of circumstance. While most people expect every conspiracy theory to link the Military Industrial Complex to the Illuminati, some are far simpler and far, far better supported by the facts.

In this book, we will examine some of those forgotten theories. We will look closely at theories that run closer to the reality of modern life. These will include some of the most important events of the last century and some seemingly more trivial theories. However, the key tenants of each case remain the same. In each, the theory posits that there had been a deliberate attempt to cover up the truth by a collection of individuals working toward a hidden and sometimes sinister goal. Read on and find out more about the world's strangest forgotten conspiracy theories.

Pearl Harbor

It could easily be argued that the attack on Pearl Harbor was one of humanity's major turning points. The events of the 7th of December, 1941 set in motion the process that would eventually lead to the dropping of mankind's most powerful weapon – the nuclear bomb – as well as set the scene for the eventual Cold War, potentially driving our species to leave the Earth for the first time and take our nascent steps on the surface of the Moon. The attack was described by the then-President Franklin D. Roosevelt as "a date that will live in infamy." The bombs that fell on the Pearl Harbor military base provided the spark that lit the fire of the American war machine in the 1940s, a fire that has not died down in the years since. With the United States armed forces being in almost perpetual conflict in one form or another ever since that day, it's easy to trace back many of the world's major wars today as emanating from that one fateful day.

Our official understanding of the attack on Pearl Harbor has become famous as one of history's preeminent surprise attacks. The story has been retold many times. At first, during the broadcasts and speeches of American politicians, then by the journalists reporting on the war, then by the history textbooks after the fight was over, and then finally by the main stream media, who turned the story into a big budget Hollywood blockbuster. Anyone who looks briefly into the attack can surmise that Japan appeared suddenly and violently at the base and left the United States with no other option than to avenge their fallen comrades and enter into the Pacific arena of the World War II.

This is what we have been officially told. For our first entry into this book of conspiracy theories, however, we will examine the possibility that there is more to the attack than meets the eye. Rather than a surprise attack, is it possible that the United States high command knew about the attack and simply let it happen, as it provided them with the perfect reason to enter into the War?

Let's start with the facts. We know that on the morning of the 7th of December, the Imperial Japanese Navy launched an attack on Pearl Harbor, the American military base in Hawaii. Arriving at 7:48 in the morning, a fleet of 353 Japanese aircraft appeared over the horizon. Among them were fighter planes, torpedo planes, and bombers, all departing from six aircraft carrying ships located some distance away. Those on the base had no idea that the Japanese were about to attack. Taken off guard, all of the eight battleships that were docked in the harbor were sunk. In all, they managed to destroy a number of very expensive ships, nearly 200 aircraft, and – most importantly – killed 2,403 American military personnel. The Japanese lost only 64 men and achieved their goal, striking a significant blow against American naval power in the Pacific.

Just as shocked as the men on the base was the rest of the American population back at home. It was only a day later that war was declared, and after dithering around the periphery of World War II, American involvement was fiercely accelerated. Any reticence that Americans might have had about intervening in the war evaporated overnight. Discussing the United States' history of isolationism, historian Braumoeller notes that domestic support skyrocketed.

Previously to Pearl Harbor, the United States had offered a form of hidden support for the Allied Powers' fight against fascism. The so-called Neutrality Patrol was just one example of this, a pact formed between the United States and the United Kingdom to establish a neutral zone in the Atlantic Ocean. While ostensibly refusing to offer outright support for either side, the Patrol offered a biased form of protection for the United Kingdom. Even if the exact phrasing of the Neutrality Patrol offered protection for all ships in neutral waters, this was of great benefit to the British. Without entering into World War II, the United States was attempting to use economic and military influence to offer support in other fashions. Among its population, citizens were split between their desire to combat the rise of the Imperial Japanese Army and the Nazis. As the preeminent world superpower, the United States was standing by and watching as Europeans smashed one another into the ground. The attack on Pearl Harbor arrived and provided the isolated power of the Americans to enter into the war. With the balance of power hurtling back and forth between the Allied and Axis powers, the arrival of the United States was a game changer.

For Japan, then, the attack seemed like a poor choice. However, this was not necessarily the case. For those in charge of the Japanese military, the disparity between the American forces and their own was stark. The attack on Pearl Harbor was not intended to beat the Americans, but rather to buy time. As discussed by L. M. Cullen and Edward Drea, the United States had long been noted as being the likely foe for Japan's future, and as early as the 1920s, plans had been made to deal with the American navy. Their strategy was to slow down the American navy and implement a "ring" defensive strategy that protected Japan by erecting outposts throughout the Pacific arena. With the American navy temporarily out of the picture, Japan could fortify and secure these posts and protect against an American invasion. Any attempt to break through the ring would incur high American causalities. The Japanese thought that these causalities would demoralize the Americans and give them pause for thought when entering into a war with America. (To say that Japan badly misunderstood and underestimated America's reaction to understate hugely. We are reminded of the quote of Japanese Admiral Soroku Yamamoto regarding the 1941 attack on Pearl Harbor which proved very appropriate. "I fear all we have done is to awaken a sleeping giant and fill him with a terrible resolve.")

The attack on Pearl Harbor, then, in their estimation, was the first step. That the Americans could eventually use their air force and atomic bombs was not accounted for in Japanese plans that were decades old. With surprise being a key element of the plan, Japan had to hope that the United States' fleet would be disabled long enough to put Japan's defenses in place.

There is a theory, however, that suggests that the American high command were not just aware of the upcoming Japanese attack, but that they welcomed it. Historians have discussed the matter at length. While the theory does remain outside the realm of typically accepted discourse, there has been a huge amount written on the subject. The argument hinges on a number of key factors.

The first of these is the possibility that the American intelligence operatives had already cracked the codes being used by the Japanese. There were two groups working on cryptanalysis at the time, the Navy's Office of Naval Intelligence (ONI) crypto group, OP-20-Gand and the Army's Signal Intelligence Service (SIS). By 1941, these groups had worked to break a number of Japan's ciphers and codes, allowing them to read a large amount of the Japanese diplomatic communications. Not all of the codes had been broken, however. Manpower was hard to come by, while the Japanese to English translators who the government trusted were worked into the ground. Irv Newman notes that the US had just over 700 people working on the codes, and that they had enjoyed some degree of success. The most important code was named JN-25 and was used by the Japanese Navy. There has been some debate as to the extent of just how many of the Japanese Navy's communications the Americans could read, but Lieutenant "Honest John" Leitwiler asserted in 1941 that he and his staff were able to "walk right across" the now readable code. Once the code was readable, it was simply a case of being able to hope that the right messages were intercepted, decrypted, and analyzed in time to make them useful.

One suggestion is that none of the messages gathered prior to December 7th mentioned Pearl Harbor specifically, but rather simply mentioned an attack on a grand scale. The messages that were gathered have not yet been declassified. Whether this is an attempt to cover up prior knowledge of the attack or the messages simply do not exist is impossible to tell. But we know the Americans could read and decrypt Japanese Navy messages. For such a large-scale attack, it seems strange to consider the surprise with which the Americans were caught.

One of the hints we get that there was at least an awareness of an upcoming attack on an American military base comes from officials from within the US government. One such person is Vice Admiral Frank E. Beatty, then an aide to the Secretary of the Navy and a part of the President's inner circle. Writing in 1954, he commented that before the attacks, it seemed obvious that the Japanese were being backed into a corner, a move constructed intentionally by President Roosevelt and Prime Minister Churchill. Beatty considers the conditions laid out to the Japanese to be so extreme that they were impossible to meet and – by setting impossible targets for the Japanese to meet in order to avoid war – made American participation in WW2 an inevitability. Another similar account comes from Henry

Stimson, who was the Secretary of War in 1941. He wrote in his diary at the time that he had held a meeting with the President and discussed the possibility of a war with Japan. In response to this, they wondered about the idea of how to best maneuver Japan into "firing the first shot" while minimizing the risk to the United States. Stimson's diaries also reveal that those in charge of Pearl Harbor were warned of an attack, and the fact that they were not ready came as some surprise to the Secretary of War. However, Stimson's diary leaves out one key part of any warning that was given to the personnel at Pearl Harbor; namely the instruction that they not warn any members of the civilian population.

Declassified in 1994, the McCollum memo is another indication that the United States wished to figure out how to arrange for Japanese provocation that would allow them to enter into the war. The memo was submitted in 1940 and broke down eight ways in which America could coerce Japan into attacking. The famous line in the document says that if "Japan could be led to commit an overt act of war, so much the better." Noted academic Gore Vidal described the memo as "the smoking gun" detailing America's intention to lure the Japanese into attacking, creating an untenable political situation that left Japan with little option but to put into action their defensive ring plan. The actions described in the memo include suggestions to give aid to China, move military forces into Dutch bases across East Asia, and embargo all trade with Japan in tandem with the British. This memo became infamous following the attack, though some have doubted whether it ever reached the office of the President. What it does tell us, however, is that there was a certain feeling within the American military that war was inevitable, that Pearl Harbor was an obvious target, and that – if possible – Japan should be encouraged to strike first and provide the pretext needed for the United States to enter the war.

The theory of the American government knowing about the attack on Pearl Harbor in advance suggests a conspiracy lurking within the intelligence community. At the heart of the theory is the suggestion that though President Roosevelt strongly desired to enter into the war, he just needed an excuse. Military historian Thomas Fleming has suggested that though Roosevelt had been encouraging Japan to strike the first blow, he had not been expecting the loss of life and infrastructure to be quite so severe. Added to this, the arrangements of treaties and alliances between Japan and Nazi Germany meant that when the US did declare war on Japan the day after the attack, Adolf Hitler was going to declare war on the United States. Having wrapped up the world in a Gordian knot of diplomatic interplays, the Pearl

Harbor attack allowed President Roosevelt to swiftly and decisively enter into the World War.

This conspiracy theory, in this instance, seems to have more than a grain of truth to it. However, it also seems to suggest that the full scale of the attack shocked the government. It was not within the plan to lose over 2000 men, but a lack of preparedness and failure to communicate between different government departments meant that the military's encouraging a Japanese attack brought forth a far greater blow than they had imagined. While it is likely the American government knew an attack was coming (and had essentially arranged for this to happen), the attack on Pearl Harbor was far worse than they had imagined. Nevertheless, their plan succeeded, and within a week, the United States was at war against the Axis powers.

The Two Babylons Theory

As we will discover throughout this book, one of the over-arching themes of the conspiracy is the concept of the clandestine, powerful organizations who are preventing the wider population from knowing the truth. This is usually a government or a corporation, but organizations don't come much larger or more powerful than the Catholic Church. For our next conspiracy, we will examine the theory that the Church has long been the front for a far more menacing purpose than you might have imagined.

After existing for nearly two millennia, it should come as no surprise that the Catholic Church has been the target for many conspiracy theories. While its power might be somewhat diminished these days, at times it has been the most powerful organization in the world. There are few forces more compelling than belief, and events such as the Crusades, the Spanish Inquisition, and La Conquista show just how much influence Catholicism has held at various points in human history.

With the fame of the Church, the story of its foundation is just as well known as the core canon of Christian mythology. Following the death of Jesus Christ, his apostles were instructed to continue his work, a process that is retold in the Bible's Acts of the Apostles. Of all his disciples, it was Peter who was chosen as the "rock" on which Jesus would build his church. According to some scholars, it was Peter who became the very first head of the Church, known as the Bishop of Rome. This position – otherwise known as the Pope – would become the leader of the Christian world for centuries. Over time, the position evolved and became refined until the Catholic Church grew into the dominant religious force in the Western world. While historians such as Oscar Cullmann, Henry Chadwick, and Raymond E. Brown have debated whether the history of the church was quite so simple, the essential lineage of the Church into the modern age is fairly accepted. Even today, the power that resides in Vatican City is obvious to anyone who visits, and the influence of both the Pope and the Church itself is still felt on a global scale.

Or so we are told. While movements such as the Reformation have cast aspersions on the religious reliability of the Catholic doctrine, others have come forward to actively accuse the Church of being set up for far more nefarious purposes. Perhaps the best known of these – and an important historical conspiracy theory – has become known as the Two Babylons theory.

The Two Babylons was the title of a pamphlet written in the 19th century by a Scottish theologian named Alexander Hislop. He was a noted member of the Scottish Presbyterian Free Church. He wrote the text in 1853, giving it the subtitle of "The Papal Worship Proved to Be the Worship of Nimrod and His Wife." It would take nearly 70 years before the piece would be published in its entirety. To put Hislop's allegations in simple terms, he accused the Catholic Church of being an organization secretly controlled by the ancient pagan religion of Babylon. The Scottish minister suggested that rather than the teachings of a man named Jesus Christ, the entire Church was simply a front for an ancient religion and the result of a conspiracy almost two thousand years old.

Though it is not as well known today, the city of Babylon was once the cultural center of the world. Located in the ancient area of Mesopotamia (current day Iraq,) it rose to a position of huge significance in the 17th Century BC. It was home to the Hanging Gardens of Babylon, one of the ancient wonders of the world and was the capital of the Babylonian Empire. At various points in its history, historians have suggested that it was the largest city in the world. Like many ancient empires, it rose to power and then eventually fell away, ultimately becoming part of the growing Muslim caliphate in the 7th century. Before then, however, it had its own complicated religion and culture.

Despite the importance of ancient Babylon on the contemporary world stage, we know relatively little of their specific religious beliefs. The idea that these belief systems influence Christianity is not limited to Hislop's work. We do know that the Babylonian religion was largely influenced by the nearby Sumerian religions, as well as the even more ancient mythology scattered around the region. What we know is from clay tablets that have been recovered. They have been translated through a number of languages and passed down, eventually reaching us today. Essentially, it is a collection of myths and legends that give us a vague outline of the belief system itself. One of the most important – Enûma Eliš – was a creation myth detailing how the Babylonians believed the world came into being. One of the religion's most noted scholars, Alfred Jeremias, has put forward the theory that these collection of myths would form the basis of the Hebrew Bible, the book that would eventually form much of the Old Testament.

Perhaps the closest parallels between the Babylonian religion and the Christian religion can be found in both Mesopotamian texts and the Book of Genesis. The idea of a shapeless void filled with nothing but water being turned by a divine creator into the world is found in both books. In Enûma Eliš, six generations of gods create the world, each of whom is associated with a specific element of the creation. This is similar to the six days taken by God to create different elements of the world in Genesis. In both texts, the seventh generation/day is associated with rest. As well as this, both the Epic of Gilgamesh and the Bible contain stories in which mankind is denied the chance of immortality due to the evil intervention of a serpent. Both of these books contain stories about the loss of humanity's innocence, as well as a great flood that killed huge numbers of the population. Further parallels between characters like Emesh and Enten with Cain and Abel have been noted, as well as the similar characteristics of the Old Testament God and the deity in the Babylonian and Sumerian texts. The influence of the ancient religions on the old Hebrew texts are undeniable, but how do they add to the theory that the Catholic Church was simply a vessel through which this religion could continue long after the death of the Babylonian culture?

Alexander Hislop begins his paper by tracing back the history of the doctrine of the Catholic Church. There is a key story in the Old Testament that actually features the city of Babylon. Hislop's journey back through the

Church leads him to the story of the Tower of Babel, whereby groups of peoples gather together and found a new city. They decide to build a tower so big it will reach heaven, a move that angers God. The deity destroys the Tower of Babel and scatters the people across the world, making it so they would never be able to understand one another's words. This is the reason given for the abundance of languages and cultures around the globe. As well as the Old Testament, the story has similar precedents in cultures throughout the Near East and Middle East. Accordingly, people have tried to associate the Tower with buildings known to have existed at the time, including structures made by Sumerians, the Egyptians, and the Babylonians.

For Hislop, however, the key association is the Tower's relationship with the biblical figure of Nimrod. Nimrod was an ancient king who has been described as a magnificent hunter. He is featured in the Bible and ancient Hebrew texts and is known as the man who was king of people who attempted to build the Tower of Babel. For centuries, people have tried to link Nimrod with actual figures from the Mesopotamia region and have described him as a Babylonian king. Hislop, however, asserts that Nimrod was worshiped as a god. He positions Nimrod as the center of the Babylonian religion and suggests that this pagan worship continued through to 0 BC and into the centuries beyond.

When reading through the Book of Revelations, Alexander Hislop associates the worship of Nimrod and the pagan religion of the Babylonians with the so-called Whore of Babylon. The Whore as described is an evil figure, one of the "Abominations of the Earth." The Whore of Babylon is one of the harbingers of the apocalypse and represents a huge, powerful, but unnamed force that exists in the world. While some people have associated the figure with the Roman Empire or Queen Elizabeth, it is Hislop's assertion that the Whore is actually the Catholic Church itself. But how does he make the leap from an ancient Babylonian king who ruled centuries before the birth of Jesus Christ to the preeminent representation of the world's most popular religion?

In the Two Babylons, Hislop puts forward his idea that the Church was not founded as a basis to spread the ideas of Jesus of Nazareth, but rather to continue the ideas that had been passed down by Nimrod. While forms of true Christianity existed and taught the lessons of Jesus (Hislop himself was a Presbyterian,) the Catholic Church was simply a vessel through which the ancient Babylonian paganism could be passed down to new generations. One of the chief allegations of Hislop's book is that the Pope (or the position of the Holy See) is actually the "lineal representative of Belshazzar," who was the last ruling king of Babylon. Before the city fell to the Persians, a message from God appeared to Belshazzar at a feast, and as described in the Book of Daniel, his paganism was converted into the religion of the Israelites. But rather than a true conversion, this worship of the pagan gods of Babylon was preserved and mixed during the foundation of the Catholic Church. While Belshazzar went into hiding following the fall of Babylon, Hislop suggests that he simply ingrained his ideas into a lineage that eventually became the highest seat of Catholicism. As such, Alexander Hislop suggests that the entire Catholic doctrine is built on a foundation of lies and misinterpretation and will only lead to the fall of Christianity.

But it is not just Babylonian paganism that Hislop traces to the church. Another of his claims relates the Egyptian gods to some of the foremost symbols and sayings of the Catholic institutions. In Catholicism, the Christogram is the three letters used to start the three names of Jesus Christ. These three letters act as a monogram, a quick way to write the name of the Catholic savior. The letters, in the language used by the Church, are IHC, standing for In Hoc Signo, meaning Jesus Savior of

Men. Hislop, however, suggests that these are simply abbreviations for the Egyptian gods Isis, Horus, and Seth. The cover is provocative, again making use of iconography to bring together the Star of David, the number of the Beast, and the word "human." Throughout, Hislop makes an effort to suggest that all Catholic ceremonies, philosophies, and doctrines are simply a conspiratorial effort to continue the pagan religion of ancient Babylon.

Despite the enduring nature of the Two Babylons theory, many modern academics have been quick to dismiss the paper. They suggest that there are many misinterpretations of both history and the Catholic religion, as well as a number of serious fabrications that take away from the believability of the piece. In particular, Ralph Woodrow's annotated version of the original text does a good job of highlighting Hislop's many errors and providing context for his claims.

That is not to say the theory is without its followers, however. It has become particularly popular among Christians of rival denominations, including Protestant fundamentalists, and had been discussed at length in The Watchtower, the most famous publication of the Jehovah's Witnesses. Even though Alexander Hislop's theory lacks the evidence required to make it a truly convincing conspiracy theory, its publication in 1919 goes to show the long history of alternative theories we have in our culture. Despite the multiple denouncements of the theory's truth, there are still a large number of people who not only know about, but believe in the theory of the Two Babylons.

The Imposed Death of the Electric Car

From one of the world's oldest institutions to the forefronts of modern technology, a conspiracy theory can cover almost every part of human culture. One of the world's largest industries (and thus its most profitable) is a primary target for the conspiracy theories of the world. The automotive industry has long been home to many dubious practices. From Henry Ford's theories of a worldwide Jewish conspiracy (see his booklet, "The International Jew") to the current Volkswagen board of directors who covered up a huge emissions scandal in favor of turning higher profits, car manufacturers have been on the wrong side of the moral fence on a number of occasions. Never has this been truer than when the nature of their business was threatened.

While we may look at companies like Tesla and see the modern day success of electric vehicles, it was not always the case. Recently, it has come to light that a cabal of automotive giants may have conspired to slow down the progress of the electric car. As detailed in the award-winning documentary "Who Killed the Electric Car?" the arrival of a working, viable electric car may well have been held up by those who already dominated the automotive industry. But how can such a huge leap forward have been suppressed for so long?

The history of the electric car is not a recent story. Rather, the attempt to create a viable, working, electric vehicle for the masses is something that has existed nearly as long as the concept of the car itself. Over the last hundred years, various electric-powered vehicles have been demonstrated, but until recently, none had truly succeeded. In their place, the internal combustion engine dominated the market and a number of huge international corporations held on to huge sectors of the market. The dominance of brands such as General Motors, Toyota, and Ford has led to the production of millions of cars every year and has resulted in billions and billions of dollars of annual profit. The fossil fuel car industry is big business, and for a number of companies, there was little inclination to change a working formula.

But the arrival of the electric car was something of an inevitability. Over the years, over 5,000 different concepts and ideas have been put forward and tested by some of the world's biggest automotive manufacturers. Factors such as the American oil crisis in the 1970s, numerous wars in the Middle East, and the acknowledgement of global warming have made the turn to renewable, more eco-friendly options inevitable; but why did it take the huge companies so long and so many attempts to create electric vehicles that actually work? To illustrate the existence of the conspiracy, the General Motors EV1 is typically used as an example.

Unlike the majority of the electric cars produced by the major automotive firms who produced electric car concepts, the EV1 actually made it to the market. It wasn't a widespread release. Instead, it was available to people in Southern California on a lease option. Part of this availability came down to a mandate passed in 1990 that required the major car companies to make electric cars available to the public as an attempt to spur their development. As such, GM, Honda, Nissan, Ford, and the other large manufacturers were forced to create and develop electric vehicles if they wanted to continue selling cars. Despite the fact that the original mandate had been passed in 1990 and had prompted the development of many electric vehicles, the conspiracy begins to emerge during the 1990s.

Gradually, the political prompts that had been designed to encourage research were steadily appealed. Though it was shielded away from the mainstream media, the California Air Resources Board was at the center of the vehicle manufacturers' efforts to push back legal efforts to bring the low emissions vehicles to market. In addition to the pressure from the lobbying groups of the automotive industry, legal work was filed again and again. As well as the car makers, representatives of the oil industry backed the legislation repeal, while representatives in the media began to build the hype for a much-mooted hydrogen car. Even though the electric cars were available, it was the futuristic hydrogen cars that were meant to be the solution. However, they were nowhere near ready. The courts were told that the electric cars were not ready, were not wanted, and that the imminent arrival of hydrogen models would be the real answer.

This is where the EV1 comes in. The EV1 was a much-maligned vehicle. Though only available in a small market, the demand for the car was incredibly low, almost to the point of being nonexistent. General Motors, one of the world's biggest car manufacturers, had released a car that was – supposedly – purposefully bad. When no one wanted the car (chiefly, because it was so bad) General Motors could take this lack of demand to the legal boards and use it as evidence that no one wanted to purchase an electric car. As such, GM took all of the EV1s back to the factory and destroyed them. In fact, the cars were recalled during their leases, much to the disapproval of the people who were driving them. These owners even organized a protest to try and stop the cars being taken from them, though GM didn't listen and had almost every single EV1 cubed. The model has become emblematic of the extent to which the automotive giants would go in order to prevent the reality of the electric car replacing their traditional internal combustion vehicles.

But why might the oil and automotive corporations enter into a conspiracy to keep the electric car from becoming a feasible prospect? As proposed in "Who Killed the Electric Car?," the oil industry faced the issue of losing out on the revenues to be gained from the wealth of public vehicles that might have been replaced by electric counterparts. Similarly, Wally Rippel suggests that the automotive manufacturers were incredibly concerned about the short term impact that the electric car projects would have on their profits, as well as any future loss to revenues that might be incurred from an unsure future. With shareholders to please, profit remained ultimate. The electric car was a threat to these profits and was accordingly seen as a threat. However, representatives from the industry itself have claimed that there was a genuine lack of interest in the vehicles produced by the companies during this era, with Dave Barthmuss suggesting that the EV1 was truly not wanted by customers and was an indication of the entire automotive market. These cars cost a lot of money and could only travel up to one hundred miles after one charge.

As well as this, the prospect of the hydrogen vehicles was very much a pipe dream. In addition to mounting legal pressures that were applied to the California Air Resources Board, a great deal of money was poured into raising awareness of the potential of hydrogen technology. These vehicles were heralded as the saviors of the not-too-distant future. These zero-emissions cars were preferable to the automotive industry as they were very much under the industry's control, but they were always still a few years from the market. As the public got more and more excited about the prospect of the hydrogen fuel cells, they soon learned to admonish the rival electric cars. Hydrogen was pushed as the answer, while the electric option was made to seem untenable in both the courts and the public's perception.

In this case, the conspiracy theory posits that the profits of the automotive and oil industries were the cause of the setback in the development of the electric car during the 1990s. Such companies controlled the car industry and felt threatened by the prospect of the new technology. In order to preserve their revenue streams, they pretended to value the development of the electric car, promoted the doomed hydrogen technology as an impending savior, and ground down the legal frameworks that were set up to try and encourage the eco-friendly alternatives. By the turn of the millennium, the gears were already in motion, and the arrival of the electric car had been suitably slowed. In collusion with government officials, the mandates requiring environmental options had been repealed, and car manufacturers were no longer required to develop such alternatives. However, while sources such as "Who Killed the Electric Car?" have been firm in their suggestions that the conspiracy exists, it is still very much a theory.

Thankfully, however, we have now reached a moment in time when the conspiracy against the electric car is no longer holding us back. Thanks to legitimate, eco-friendly options such as the Toyota Prius and the Tesla Roadster, we now have actual vehicles that are not only available for the public to purchase but really do work. Even with the automotive and oil industries turning huge profits in the modern age, the age of the conspiracy against the electric car seems to have passed. The only question that remains is just how much damage we have done to the environment in the time since the conspiracy first began. With the conspiracy having been set back for potentially twenty years, climate change could well have been greatly slowed down had the internal combustion already been consigned to the scrap heap. In this instance, the conspiracy may have actually done serious harm to the planet as a whole.

Garry Kasparov versus Deep Blue

Not every conspiracy involves global conglomerates attempting to dictate to the world the direction humanity will take. In some instances, it can be pride as well as profits that cause people to enter into and conspire in a conspiracy. In certain situations, some people may choose to subvert and alter the true nature of things for their own personal gain. In the case of Garry Kasparov versus the chess computer, Deep Blue, the computer manufacturer IBM has been accused of cheating the renowned grandmaster out of his legitimate victory.

The story of Garry Kasparov versus the machine can be read as a steady parallel to the development of the personal computer. In the early 1990s, as more and more people were becoming familiar with the idea of just how powerful and useful computers could be, IBM was one of the major dominant forces in the world of computing. Despite one-time IBM chairman Thomas Watson predicting that "I think there is a world market for maybe five computers," the rise of the machines in the workplace and the home brought with it an increased awareness of what they were actually capable of. In accordance, it was felt that a public display of the computing strength would be a boost for IBM and would allow them to demonstrate the capabilities of their machines. In order to achieve the maximum impact, they recruited famed chess grandmaster Garry Kasparov and challenged him to a game.

Chess is one of the world's oldest games. There are a near-infinite number of ways in which a game can pan out, and the playing of the game is not just a process of weighing up the suitability of every single move at one possible moment. As well as the rules and the history of the game, any computer attempting to play chess would need to comprehend strategy and tactics in an intelligent manner. Not only this, but they would need to implement these qualities when coming up against one of the best players in the world. While rudimentary chess programs had been created many decades earlier, IBM created a dedicated supercomputer purely for the 1989 match against Kasparov. They christened it "Deep Thought," named for the computer in Douglas Adams's famed series, "The Hitchhikers' Guide to the Galaxy."

The first match between Garry Kasparov and Deep Thought passed by as many assumed such a match would. The human player beat the computer with a fair degree of comfort, but was quick to praise the engineers and programmers of the machine for their ability to present him with something of a challenge. Never one to shy away from publicity, Kasparov emerged from the bout with a heightened media profile, while the IBM employees soon decided to reinvent their machine to better take on the chess player. In doing so, they created Deep Blue, playing on IBM's colloquial nickname of Big Blue, and worked with another grandmaster, Joel Benjamin, to redesign the way the computer approached the openings of the game. IBM faced their new baby up against alternative computers and fixed, fiddled, and bumped up the capabilities of the machine until they once again felt that they might be able to take on Kasparov.

The key conspiracy theory revolves around the next two games. The first of these was played in 1996 and, for a while, it seemed that the machine had been raised up to a surprisingly good level. While the Russian grandmaster won three of the games and drew two, the IBM machine became the first computer to ever win a game of chess against the reigning world champion. The series of games lasted a week, and it was clear to the audience that this match-up was far more challenging to Kasparov than the earlier series of games. Just over a year later, the combatants were set to face one another once again.

During this intervening period, IBM took the time to perform some heavy upgrades to their machine. Taking on Gary Kasparov in May of 1997, the machine this time emerged victorious. After six games, the computer led the world champion by 3.5 to 2.5. In winning the sixth game, IBM's creation became the first computer program to triumph over a reigning world champion in a standard match. This ability came not wholly from the refined programming knowledge and abilities of the computer, but mostly from the brute force abilities its computing architecture provided. As one of the most powerful supercomputers on the planet, it could consider the potential of up to 200 million different moves every single second. This was twice as powerful as the computer Kasparov had beaten a year earlier. When planning ahead in the game, Deep Blue would typically think up to eight moves ahead, and had the ability to consider nearly twenty moves in advance. The program was designed not simply to win, but to evaluate the state of the board at any given moment. Should it protect the king? Should it try and capitalize on a space advantage in the center? Should it attempt to orchestrate additional space in a different area of the board? While these processes might seem instinctual to the human chess player, they had to be written into the code of the machine.

As well as this programming, Deep Blue was loaded with the exact details of thousands of games between the greatest chess grandmasters. Although the computer could analyze these move sets for patterns and ideas, the machine was incapable of truly creative, original play. The knowledge loaded into the machine was refined by not only Joel Benjamin, but also by a further group of grandmasters, including Nick de Firmian, John Fedorowicz, and Miguel Illescas. While the computer was loaded with nearly 700,000 older games (including those by Kasparov,) any requests from the grandmaster that he be allowed access to the computer's previous matches were denied. Instead, Kasparov had to turn to other computer programs in order to try and get an understanding of how a machine might play. The machine, said IBM, had been programmed to win chess matches. The victory over Kasparov was proof of their ability to build and program incredibly complex and cutting edge computers.

But Garry Kasparov was not pleased. The aftermath of the match in 1997 was not pleasant. Instead of being beaten by a machine, the grandmaster claimed to have noticed examples of truly deep intelligence behind the computer's moves. Instead of brute force computing, he claimed to have seen examples of creativity in its play that were not present in the earlier matches. It was his assertion that he had not played against a machine. Instead, he had come up against both the machine and its creators, who had intervened in the game. This, were it proven to be true, would be a clear violation of the rules that both parties had agreed to before the match took place. Kasparov was certain that a conspiracy was in place to guarantee the machine victory and provide IBM with a triumph over the reigning world champion.

In order to chase down his accusations, Kasparov requested that he be provided with the log files from the machine. The developers of Deep Blue were allowed to make changes to the programs between games in order to address weaknesses and issues that arose during play. When Kasparov requested the printout of these changes, he was again denied. Though these files would eventually be published on the internet, the fact that they were denied to the grandmaster only further cemented his theory. The Russian demanded a rematch (as he himself had granted IBM) but again, IBM flatly refused and even went as far as dismantling the computer following the match.

For Kasparov, one of the key moments of the game and part of the foundation for his case against the company was a strange move that occurred in the first game. The 44th move shocked Kasparov during the game, as it seemed to him to be the result of true intelligence and unlike anything the machine had played in any of the prior games. The grandmaster's mind stuck on this move, and he suggested that the anxiety and concern that it prompted resulted in a drop in his abilities to perform in the next game. For writer Nate Siler, this move was the result of a bug in the software that IBM wrote and was not intentional. For Kasparov, it was the key piece of evidence to show that the machine was not playing alone.

In a documentary produced about the controversial game, entitled "Game Over: Kasparov and the Machine," the filmmakers conducted a number of interviews in which the idea of IBM's stock price is mentioned. With all of the publicity surrounding the match, the opportunity to finally beat a human world champion at the game of chess resulted in a boost to the stock price of the computer company and inflated their value by millions of dollars. This was enough of a motivation to interfere with the programming of the computer, with only a slight change and a slight breaking of the rules being sufficient to disrupt Kasparov's regular game. This slight intervention by the designers of the machine was enough to boost stock prices by a huge margin and provided a decent motivation to enter into a conspiracy against the Russian grandmaster.

Garry Kasparov versus Deep Blue has become a world famous event. The immediate refusal of the computer firm to deny the grandmaster any chance of a rematch meant that it was the final chapter in the succession of games between IBM's machines and Kasparov. At first glance, it seems as though gradual improvements and raw computing power were eventually enough to overcome the world champion at his own game and to cement IBM's position as the leading manufacture of powerful supercomputers on the world stage.

But it is not quite so simple. As Garry Kasparov himself has maintained, the tiny details do not add up. Forced into a corner and denied the chance to study the computer's game beforehand, Kasparov came up against an unknown foe. When this foe began to act erratically and display elements of truly creative intelligence, it was enough to trigger warning signs in Kasparov's mind. These played upon his thoughts and proved to be enough to lead to his downfall. It is his theory that the designers of Deep Blue conspired against him in an effort to prove the company's value on the world stage. With so much money and influence at stake, the small details – the refusal of access to the log files, the denial of a rematch, the immediate dismantling of the machine – all added up to an increased level of suspicion by Garry Kasparov and his supporters.

As with many conventional conspiracy theories, the deeper one delves, the less and less the accusations begin to look as though they stem from simple paranoia. With a great deal to gain from a potential victory, what was to prevent IBM from slightly turning the tide in their favor? Though these accusations have long been forgotten while the results of the match live on, it's important to consider the truth behind the battle between man and machine.

Chemtrails

One continued convention in the world of conspiracy theories is to seize on the incredibly familiar and to try and discover the true, ulterior motive behind the mundane. One of the best examples of this is the conspiracy theories that suggest that "chemtrails" may be far more sinister than you might ever have imagined. For those unaware, a chemtrail is the trail left through the sky when a jet plane or airliner passes overhead. Look up on any given day, and you may well see many examples of these trails as they crisscross the sky. But whereas conventional knowledge will suggest that these are the by-product of the engines used by the planes, the conspiracy theory posits that they are in fact chemical or biological products that are being spread across the unsuspecting public by the government. As far as typical conspiratorial paranoia goes, it ranks among the most paranoid theories around and is also one of the most popular.

Conventional wisdom from the scientific community has dismissed the theories surrounding the supposed chemtrails. The theory suggests that the contrails normally left by high flying aircraft are quick to dissipate and those that linger in the sky are in fact filled with chemicals or biological agents which the public are not told about. However, the generally held response to these conspiratorial claims is that these are typical water-based trails that one should expect to be left behind. Dependent on the atmospheric conditions present at any given time, the existence of the trails is to be entirely expected. It then falls on the proponents of the theory to prove that the chemtrails are spread with malicious intent with the majority of people happy to accept the conventional wisdom regarding these phenomena.

Perhaps it helps to start our investigation with an explanation of the word chemtrails itself. The word is what is known as a portmanteau, a combination of "chemical" and "trail." It follows on from the word "contrail," which is a similar combination of "condensation" and "trail." This gives us an indication of the key issue believers have with the idea of chemtrails – namely, that the condensation one might expect has been replaced by some kind of nefarious chemical. Spread from a height of some five to ten miles, these chemicals could well have numerous purposes. Suggested theories have included everything from population control to the management of solar radiation. The conspiracy theory is complex in that it does not have one agreed upon function for the use of chemicals. So whether they're designed to control the weather, control people, or spread psychological warfare, how did people come to suspect the contrails?

Researchers have traced the theories about chemtrails back to 1996. At this time, the United States Air Force had been accused of spreading "mysterious substances" across the country and spraying the population of the United States. People had noticed that the patterns of their aircraft had been producing "unusual" contrails and contrail patterns. In response, the Air Force simply claimed that these accusations were unsubstantiated and the result of a hoax. They followed many of the accusations back to a paper published at the military's own Air University, a paper that was concerned with the potential to control the weather in any given theater of war. The paper suggested that, by 2025, the Air Force might be able to alter the weather conditions in battle zones in order to gain an advantage. Though it was a real strategic paper, the government agencies have reiterated many times that it was based on fictional theorizing of potential futures and future technologies. They went even further to confirm that such strategies were not under legitimate consideration, nor were they possible with current technology. As well as this, the Air Force – clearly perturbed by the suggestion that they might be involved in such practices – went a step further in order to confirm that the majority of the scientists they consulted were prepared to confirm the benign nature of the contrails seen in the skies over America.

However, as with any good conspiracy theory, a government simply denying the possibility of something being true was not nearly enough for a theory like chemtrails to be rejected. The publication Skeptical Inquirer (which prides itself on looking closely at alternative truths) suggested that the idea of chemtrails became popular during the 1990s but quickly spread across late night radio shows and through the work of journalists such as William Thomas. It was, they acknowledged, something that was rarely mentioned in the mainstream media outlets.

But it was not an exclusively American theory. In the United Kingdom, politicians were being asked similar questions. The first of these questions directly asked the government what it was doing to combat the possibility of the polluting effects of these aircraft. In response, the Secretary of State working for the department of Environment, Food, and Rural Affairs simply stated that they planned to conduct no such investigations, simply because the phenomena were not widely recognized by scientists the world over. They did, however, admit that some research was being done into the nature of contrails, though there was little in the way of results that were worth mentioning at this time. Similar questions were put to the Canadian government, with individuals concerned about the effect of "aerial sprayings" and how they might affect the public. Again, they were told by government officials that there was no evidence for the idea that "high altitude spraying" was taking place in Canada. In almost every instance, there was the insistence that the members of the public were seeing normal, non-threatening contrails and mistaking them for the supposed chemtrails they had heard about.

Since then, numerous governments across the world have reiterated the idea that chemtrails do not exist or that the contrails that people do see are not harmful. But there exists a small subset of the population that believes otherwise. Though there is not an overriding consensus on the matter, there are a number of ideas that are agreed upon. The first of these is that contrails and chemtrails can be recognized as different, even from the ground. Unlike contrails, the chemical equivalent will linger in the air for much longer. These can stay around for up to twelve hours or can even dissolve into something resembling a normal cirrus cloud formation. One common proclamation is that the chemtrails as they first emerged in the mid-1990s were slightly different and stayed even longer in the sky.

The chemical makeup of the chemtrails has been discussed at length in the conspiracy community. There have been suggestions that barium, polymer fibers, aluminum salts, or thorium can be found in the residue, while others have suggested that the trails are conduits for a hugely powerful electromagnetic weapon. Each individual's theory regarding the chemical composition of the chemtrails typically depends on what the individual's particular reasoning as to the motivations for their use. Weapons testing, population control, and weather modification all dictate that different chemicals or biological agents must be used by the government. Putting together a firm picture of the composition of the chemtrails is almost impossible, as it would involve coming to a general consensus on the purpose of the phenomena. In order to delve deeper into their purpose, it might help to think about the evidence that does exist.

Aside from the continued assertion that the chemtrails exist, the most famous pieces of evidence are the photographs that purport to show the insides of passenger aircraft with large barrels placed where the seats are usually found. With wires and tubes coming out of the barrels, proponents of the theory claim that this is a documented example of the production of chemtrails. However, this has been countered by the aviation industry, who claim that the purpose of the barrels is to simulate and approximate the weight of passengers during the testing phase of a plane's development. The barrels are filled with water, which is then pumped between the barrels in order to test various centers of gravity.

Another commonly cited piece of evidence is a television report broadcast in 2007 by a news program in Louisiana. During the piece, a supposed section of a chemtrail is tested and found to be containing higher than normal levels of barium, at almost three times the limit allowed by the US government. However, critics point out that the testing equipment was not used correctly, and thus exaggerated the findings and threw the results off by a factor of 100. As such, the levels of barium were indeed safe.

One of the strangest pieces of evidence was made famous thanks to Congressman Dennis Kucinich. In 2001, Kucinich brought the Space Preservation Act of 2001 to the attention of Congress. It should be noted that he did not author the piece, but merely introduced it. Had the act passed, it would have banned the possibility of the government basing weapons in space at any point in the future. Among the examples listed in the literature were chemtrails, described as an "exotic" weapon, among the types that would be banned. For believers in the conspiracy theory, this piece of legislation is seen as an official acknowledgement by the government that such chemtrails do exist and that they could be used as weapons. The same bill, however, does mention other exotic weapons, including those which are "extraterrestrial" and "tectonic." Nevertheless, the bill was not met favorably and failed to pass. All future attempts to pass a similar bill, it has been noted, did not include "chemtrails" in their wording. For believers, this was only further proof that the inclusion in the document was an acknowledgement by the government of the existence of the rogue contrails.

Trying to pin down an accurate depiction of the theory about chemtrails is difficult. Due to their very nature, they are hard to examine up close, can be attributed to anything, and any amount of evidence against their existence always comes from those who are firmly rooted within the system itself. As such, they are an example of the classic conspiracy language whereby the theory can mean a huge amount to many, many different people. The huge amount of science and research we have concerning jet planes in the atmosphere simply points to contrails being a benign phenomenon. But for anyone who seeks to prove their particular theory correct, the concept of chemtrails can be molded and altered to fit pre-existing stereotypes.

For example, we know that contrails are formed when water vapor is emitted from piston and jet engines at extreme altitudes, with the vapor then condensing and forming a cloud. The hot air emitted by the engines mixes with the exterior cold air to form contrails and, depending on the prevailing weather conditions, they may stay in the sky for extended periods of time. All of the research that has been conducted and published to this point indicates that this is to be expected and is simply the result of typical aviation travel.

Instead, however, the chemtrails give those with keen imaginations the perfect canvas on which to project their ideas. Contrails are familiar to the majority of people, while at the same time few people can explain the exact mechanics behind their appearance and their lingering in the sky. So when presented with two alternative theories – that they are simply by-products of air travel or that they are part of a larger conspiracy – the second idea can seem much more interesting and exciting. In situations like this, it can be typical human nature to favor that which we find to be more entertaining and which also can be used to explain various other conspiracies from across the world.

But Bob Berman, an astronomer, raises a good point about the chemtrails. It is his assertion that this is the perfect situation in which to apply "Occam's razor." Occam's razor is a philosophical tool that suggests that when presented with two competing ideas, you should always favor the one that is based on the fewest assumptions. This favoring of the "simplest" solution would suggest that the idea of a global, complicated, and fairly recent conspiracy to douse the world with chemical using jet planes is less likely than the idea that contrails are simply produced during regular flights. In this respect, solving the mystery of the chemtrails is often a case of wondering whether there really is a mystery at all.

Was AIDS constructed as a weapon?

Chemtrails are not the first time a conspiracy theory has revolved around the government unleashing chemical weapons on its own population. One of the most pervasive theories of modern times relates to the emergence and terrifying effects of the AIDS virus during the last five decades. Arriving in the public consciousness with incredible urgency and seemingly out of nowhere, this hideously deadly disease swept through countries and communities to devastating effect. As a means of trying to explain why this disease had arrived so suddenly, some people turned towards the idea that it had been created by man with the intention of being exactly this lethal. Only man, they suggested, could truly create a plague so dangerous. This has led to the enduring theory that HIV and the AIDS virus were created as a weapon before being unleashed upon the world.

The world has experienced terrible diseases before. During the Middle Ages, the Black Death destroyed huge swathes of the population of Europe, Asia, and anywhere else it could reach. Epidemics like the Spanish Flu have, as recently as the early twentieth century, shown just how unprepared we might be for the sudden emergence of a deadly new disease. But in recent times, the best example of a previously unheard of illness that has caused such utter destruction is AIDS.

The disease arrived seemingly out of the blue. It was technically discovered in the 1980s by a French researcher. But it was the effects upon certain communities that brought it to the realization of the public. Transmitted sexually or intravenously, it made its way quickly through certain demographics such as homosexual communities and drug users. These smaller communities on the fringe of society soon saw themselves wiped out. Quickly, news reports picked up on the epidemic. It was a disease without a cure, one that killed those who contracted the virus with seemingly a 100% mortality rate. There was confusion over how the disease would be spread and over who might have it. To say that AIDS scared people would be an understatement. Even outside of the communities most obviously affected, there was a fear and a confusion about just how quickly it might spread and who might be safe.

To start with, let us understand the current theory of the development of AIDS. *Acquired immunodeficiency syndrome*, to give the disease its full name, affects those who have contracted the human immunodeficiency virus, otherwise known as HIV. In researching the history of AIDS, we must look to the history of HIV. The virus has been traced to a very similar virus found in simians in West Central Africa. Whether it evolved or is simply closely related (or was even purposefully modified,) we do not know. What we are aware of, however, is that simian immunodeficiency virus (SIV) is the key to understanding the history of AIDS and how it came to infect humans. Scientists now suggest that the virus spread out from West Central Africa sometime in the last century and, just as viruses are wont to do, began to spread its dangerous influence wider and wider.

But for a long time, the arrival of AIDS seemed like a plague from some divine being. Religious figures were quick to try and blame the morality of the fringe members of society who seemed most prone to contracting the disease, while others were happy to ignore the suffering simply because they were not among the most at-risk demographics. In situations like this, misinformation and rumor spread like wildfire. Either the rumors and theories were emerging from among the affected communities themselves and seemed to offer hope for some sort of cure, or they were told as ghost stories by the unaffected portions of society almost as a warning to not stray too far into the fringe elements of society. This context was ripe for the emergence of one of America's most enduring conspiracy theories.

For more information on the idea that AIDS was created in a lab and purposefully unleashed upon the population, it can help to turn to Phil Watson, who is the executive director of the Black AIDS Institute located in Los Angeles. One of the communities most affected by the spread of disease was the African American demographic. With large amounts of the population economically disadvantaged after years of segregation and racial divisions within the country, there were higher rates of intravenous drug use, less funding for sex education classes in inner city communities, and continued subjugation from the law enforcement communities. With a history as one of the most persecuted sectors of American society, the African American community was hugely at risk from the spread of the disease. When discussing current views of the virus, Phil Watson's Institute went out and interviewed 500 black Americans. Their findings indicated that, of those surveyed, almost half believed that the disease was created by man. A quarter of these people felt that the disease was created in a laboratory controlled by the government and, of the 500 people interviewed, at least twelve suggested that AIDS had been created by the CIA. As well as this, over half of the people thought that any kind of cure for the disease was purposefully withheld from poor communities. Just under half believed that any new drugs that were released were simply tests in which the government used the population as guinea pigs. AIDS, for 15% of people, was a kind of genocide unleashed upon the people.

The African American community's view of AIDS is similar in effect to the idea that crack cocaine was purposefully created by the CIA as a form of population control and purposefully spread by Ronald Reagan's Republican government to subdue and demonize black communities. The view of AIDS as a weapon has many institutional backers. The Nation of Islam promotes the view that the virus was created by the government, who have colluded with pharmaceutical companies in order to commit genocide. Reverend Jeremiah Wright, a leading figure in certain communities, has also put forward similar theories and quotes Leonard Horowitz in discussions of AIDS having been created as a weapon.

One of the most important pieces of evidence comes from Wangari Maathai, who was a Nobel Peace Prize laureate noted for his environmental activism in 2004. When being interviewed by Time magazine, Wangari was asked about his views on AIDS as a manufactured disease. He reiterated his beliefs that AIDS was a "biological weapon" designed and created by members of developed nations with the express purpose of eliminating black peoples. He did acknowledge that he had "no idea" who actually created the disease, and later retracted a large portion of his comments, stating that he did not believe that AIDS was created by white people to destroy African people.

Despite the prevalence of these beliefs in certain communities, society at large seems quick to dismiss the idea of AIDS as being created in a laboratory, but is the concept that far flung? Recently declassified intelligence reports have detailed experiments that were taking place in Los Alamos, Cold Spring Harbor, and Fort Detrick as early as 1910. Titled "Common Genetic Alterations of RNA," the experiments involved scientists mixing combinations of extant diseases such as the maeda-visna virus found in sheep and the bovine leukemia virus. An outbreak of the former hit Iceland over the course of two decades between 1930 and 1950 and killed every single sheep. But neither virus is harmful to humans. In fact, only a few strains of viruses have leaped between species. These tend to be the truly dangerous ones, such as Yellow Fever, Dengue Fever, or Lassa fever. Nevertheless, these animal viruses were purposefully injected into human tissue samples, and the process repeated until the virus themselves mutated, eventually incorporating human genes.

Experiments such as these show the willingness to test and experiment on the tenable nature of diseases affecting humans. Biological warfare, though now chiefly outlawed by international treaty, was once big business. During the Cold War, the competition with the Soviets not only meant that America needed to better understand disease when compared to their communist counterparts, but should the worst come to the worst, they should have the upper hand in any form of warfare. An incurable, quick-spreading disease would be the ideal way in which to infect a large portion of the population without the need to destroy infrastructure that might be damaged during, for example, a nuclear strike. The various peaks and troughs of the Cold War had usually provided America with a theater in which to test its various new weapons. The close of the World War II had kick-started the nuclear age, with the United States dropping atomic bombs on Nagasaki and Hiroshima in clear view of the Russians. Likewise, the war in Vietnam had provided the Americans with the chance to test chemical weapons such as the infamous Agent Orange. But by the time the 1980s rolled around and Ronald Reagan had taken charge of the country, the existence of a large scale testing theater of such magnitude was simply not there. Instead, so the conspiracy theory goes, Reagan and the Pentagon decided to launch AIDS into the poorest areas of the country and studied its effects.

As mentioned earlier, the theory of crack cocaine being similarly used as a means of population control during the time is not dissimilar. The theory of crack being introduced by the CIA into African American communities runs alongside Reagan's War on Drugs, which would eventually prove to be disastrous and would result in the incarceration of a huge number of black Americans on relatively minor drug charges. While crack was an addictive substance that got its users hooked, AIDS was a silent killer which moved from needle to needle. If we are to believe the conspiracy theories, the perilous effects of crack cocaine and AIDS arriving in America almost in tandem had a devastating effect on the country's poorest communities.

Trying to prove that AIDS was created in a lab, however, is a difficult task. With the majority of evidence pointing towards an emergence from West Central Africa, some have suggested that after being developed in the early part of the century, it was eventually planted in a foreign country in order to better distance the United States from blame when the disease finally emerged. But as we have eventually discovered the involvement of the CIA in numerous drug deals with cartels throughout South America in the 1970s and 1980s, we may one day find the smoking gun that links one of the world's most deadly diseases to the Pentagon. As technology advances, this may well be found coded into the virus itself and could even lead to a cure being discovered.

Until that day, however, the theory that AIDS was developed as a weapon and used on the fringe members of American society remains very much a theory.

The Lost Cosmonauts

The space race between the United States and the USSR during the 1950s, 1960s, and 1970s is the source of many of the most well-known conspiracy theories. Perhaps the greatest of all is the idea that the moon landing was faked and that Buzz Aldrin and Neil Armstrong never set foot on the surface of the moon. As one of the most enduring conspiracy theories, there are still television shows, books, and articles being produced to this day which entertain the idea. But the space race involved two parties. As well as the Americans, the Soviets also produced their own strange tales. Among these is the idea of the failed space flights. Otherwise known as the Lost Cosmonauts theory, it suggests that a number of people died as the Soviets attempted to put a man into orbit but their deaths were covered up by the government in order to maintain their reputation.

Anyone who has studied the travails and achievements of both sides of the space race will know that a Russian man named Yuri Gagarin is commonly credited as the first man in space. However, the conspiracy theory suggests that rather than being the first man to enter space, he was simply the first to survive. According to the theory, there were at least two men who proceeded him who did not make it back to Earth. As well as the two deaths, there have been suggestions that a third cosmonaut misjudged his entry and found himself having landed in China. Together, they are known as the lost cosmonauts.

The idea of the lost Soviet spacemen is not recent. Rather, it can be traced back as far as 1959. In December of that year, high ranking members of the communist regime in Czechoslovakia released a series of leaks which seemed to include a number of unofficial shots of space. These documents included the name Aleksei Ledovsky, who, it was suggested, had been sent into space inside an R-5A rocket the Russian scientists had converted. He was not thought to have survived. As well as Ledovsky, three more names of men and women were included. These leaks backed up information that had come from a space theoretician named Hermann Oberth, who had told stories of a man being killed during a sub-orbital flight in 1958. Of the world's news groups, only an Italian agency named Continentale picked up on the Czech stories and reported the deaths. While they were able to name the supposedly dead cosmonauts, they were not able to confirm Oberth's theory of the deadly sub-orbital flight.

The next spate of deaths involved a group of high altitude parachutists. Colonel Pyotr Dolgov, Ivan Kachur, and Alexey Grachov all had their photos published in a 1959 issue of Ogoniok but would die over the coming years. They were thought to have been involved in the testing of extreme high altitude equipment, including Sokol pressure suits that would be direct ancestors of those used in Soviet space flights. While Dolgov is known to have died in action, Kachur simply disappeared shortly after. Another man, Gennady Zavadovsky, was also pictured with the parachutists. He, too, disappeared before his name eventually appeared on a list of dead cosmonauts long after, with no details of the exact nature of his death, nor the date. High altitude parachutists had often been rumored as the precursors to the Soviet cosmonauts. Used to the extreme altitudes, they were the perfect candidates to test the equipment as the Russians climbed higher and higher into the atmosphere. During the 1960s, both Yaroslav Golovanov, a Russian journalist and the New York Journal-American published investigations into the parachutist's involvement in the cosmonaut program, which eventually proved that they had never quite reached space. Even if they were the precursors to the cosmonauts, any of those who died could not have been said to have done so on the way into or on the way back from space.

One of the most famous pieces of evidence in this conspiracy comes from the two brothers who operated amateur radio equipment during the 1960s. The Judica-Cordiglia brothers produced what have become known as the Torre Bert recordings, which in turn seemingly support the theory that some of the Russian cosmonauts did not make it back to Earth. The two brothers had repeatedly suggested that they have audio recordings of a number of space programs conducted by the Soviets during the 1960s. They suggest that the recordings detail the tragic end of a number of failed launches. The mysterious nature of these recordings has sparked the public's interest for more than five decades, though there have been a number of rebuttals that have doubted the veracity of the tapes and the content they appear to detail. Despite the seemingly shocking content of the last few minutes of the cosmonauts' lives, others are seemingly not convinced. The audio quality and the accents of the voices have both been cited as reasons as to why they might not be entirely what the brothers claim them to be.

One of the early cosmonauts for whom we do seem to have more evidence for is a man named Vladimir Ilyushin. Ilyushin was the son of a noted Soviet aeronautic designer and went on to become one of the country's top pilots. It is thought by some that he was actually the first man sent into space, supposedly on the 7th of April, 1961, days before Yuri Gagarin made his famous flight. The theories about Ilyushin's flight suggest that when it came to the landing, he was force to crash far from the intended descent zone. Instead of arriving back in Russia, he found himself in Chinese territory. He was immediately captured by the local authorities and spent a year under their careful eye before being sent back to Russia. Because this failure would have been deemed as embarrassing to the Soviet space program, it is suggested that they chose to downplay the important of the flight and to instead promote Gagarin's flight as being the first, a flight which took place five days later.

But this part of the theory is not without evidence. A British journalist named Dennis Ogden was working in Russia as a correspondent for a communist newspaper in his home country and managed to gather together details of Ilyushin treatment at the hands of the Chinese medical staff. Soviet sources, meanwhile, have always positioned Ilyushin as a great test pilot but never a man who was considered a cosmonaut. The official line includes the detail that Ilyushin was seriously injured in a car accident in 1960, and in order to mend his broken legs, was sent to China to receive traditional treatment unavailable in Russia at the time. However, the theory was given new life in 1999 when the son of Nikita

Khrushchev, Sergei, appeared in a documentary named "The Cosmonaut Cover Up," wherein he suggested that Ilyushin had been held in China after a crashed space flight. Its Sergei's supposition that by the time Ilyushin arrived back in Russia, the Gagarin legend was already well established enough that it was impossible to dislodge, nor was it deemed necessary to tell the public the truth about the captured cosmonaut. As a further point, any potential schism between the communist powers of the USSR and China was to be hidden from the eyes of the west. Ilyushin died in 2010 and never confirmed or denied the theory about him actually being the first man in space.

But if Ilyushin managed to make it into space and was denied the opportunity to revel in the legend of being the first human to do so, there may well have been other cover-ups that had more disastrous ends. These allegations suggest that, while attempting to reach the moon, a conspiracy covered up the death of a number of Soviet cosmonauts who were lost in space. As we know today, the USSR would lose the race with America to be the first to reach the moon. However, the American flight that first reached the desired destination – Apollo 11 – was not working in isolation. It has been suggested that a number of days before the American launch, the Soviets held a launch of their own.

Up to this point, the USSR's rockets had not been working exactly as planned. Despite this lack of success, it is suggested that the decision to launch a manned mission was taken nevertheless, with the hope of beating the Americans to the destination by a matter of days. Taking place on the 3rd of July, 1969, the N1 rocket exploded on the launch pad. Everyone on board was killed. However, official statements denied that it had been intended to launch a manned mission and was simply another test flight.

When it became clear that the Americans had won the race to the moon, the Soviet programs began to take on a less urgent tone. The ideological battle played out in the race to outer space had caused both countries to take an intense approach to scientific advancement. Huge amounts of time and money had been ploughed into both space programs in a show of strength as the world two foremost superpowers faced off against one another on the world stage. Just as there were rumors that the Soviets were losing men in space, the Americans too experienced the tragedy of the death of their astronauts. As well as the fabled Apollo 13 mission in which three men nearly died, the men aboard Apollo 1 – Roger Chaffee, Virgil Grissom, and Edward White – were burned to death during a training exercise when their cabin caught fire. Unlike the USSR, however, it has been easier to confirm and document these events; historians and conspiracy theorists have not had to try and navigate the complexity of the Soviet state's ability to keep secrets.

But the conspiracy theories also took on a biased tone. One of the most popular American equivalents of the stories suggests that the men recruited into the cosmonaut program were willing to throw away their lives for the good of the state. It has been suggested that those who came aboard the Luna program willingly entered into a suicide pact and were entirely happy to face their demise for the betterment of the Soviet's understanding of the space race. These suicide missions were so doomed that the flights did not include life support machines for the men aboard. Because this was deemed to be extra weight, the men were simply sent up into space to operate their machinery, before they would eventually pass away. It became politically advantageous for the American public to believe that the Soviet Union valued human life so little that they were willing to send their cosmonauts to their death (whereas the American astronauts were treated as heroes), but there remains little evidence for these beyond the concept being mentioned in the book, Omon Ra, by Pelevin, a Russian fiction writer.

Despite the lack of evidence for anything other than the captured cosmonaut who spent a year in China, the idea of the doomed Soviet space flights has certainly caught the public's attention. The theory has worked its way into books, plays, and films. The image of a doomed man floating high above the Earth is both chilling and the height of science fiction. As the space race seemed so important in the day to day life of the 1950s and 1960s, the conspiracy theory of Russia's lost cosmonauts only worked to better the image of the American space program. Despite the fact that they had succeeded in putting a man into space before anyone else, the suggestions and rumors of the dead cosmonauts could be seen as a deliberate attempt to denigrate and discredit the Russians' efforts. As with everything during the Cold War, the ideological battle was ingrained far deeper than we might be able to imagine today.

In most conspiracy theories, attempting to find real, hard evidence can be almost impossible. While we are sometimes looking to clandestine governments and corporations for the smoking gun, trying to extract such information from the behemoth of secrecy that was the Soviet Union is almost impossible. When you factor in the manner in which the USSR collapsed, it might be a long time indeed before someone is able to finally uncover the truth behind the Soviet space program. The only other method would be to journey out into the cold depths of space and check every single vessel for the remains of the lost Russian cosmonauts as they continue to orbit the Earth.

The Phantom Time Hypothesis

After the seriousness of the lost cosmonauts, it can be helpful to examine the idea that conspiracy theories can be a little bit more abstract. While they typically entail a shadowy scheme to exploit a large group of people, there are theories that can seem to be far stranger. One of these is the "phantom time hypothesis."

First put forward by the German writer and historian Heribert Illig, the theory suggests that there has been a huge error in our dating system. More specifically, the period between 614 AD and 911 AD simply does not exist. This part of the Early Middle Ages was instead fabricated, with anything said to have happened during this time being either equally as fabricated or simply having occurred earlier. According to Illig, we have a gap in our calendar of nearly 300 years. As a means of explanation, Illig suggests that the period was inserted into the calendar as the result of a millennium-old conspiracy.

The theory begins with the head of the Holy Roman Empire, Otto III, as he collaborates with the man who was head of the Catholic Church at the time, Pope Sylvester II. It may even have included the leader of the Byzantine Empire, Constantine VII, but the chief protagonists remains the Holy Roman Emperor and the Pope. It is Illig's assertion that the pair colluded together to alter the known date and to bring them closer to the year 1000 AD. At the same time, it permitted them the ability to invent three centuries of history. One of their most famous inventions would be Charlemagne. They were to accomplish this with a campaign of misrepresentation, forgery, alerting of documents, and the construction of physical evidence. Were this theory to be true, the year 2010 would actually be 1713, 2015 would be 1718, and so on. If Illig is correct, then we are still very much in the eighteenth century.

But while the theory might seem to be incredibly outlandish (how is it possible to simply conjure up 300 years of history?), Illig does strive to bring evidence to the table. It is in this respect that the phantom time hypothesis is truly one of the most notable conspiracy theories around – if it were proved to be true, it would entail a secretive collusion of epic proportions. Simply by dint of the hypothesis it advances, it is worthy of looking deeper into the reasons as to why we might possibly have lost three hundred years of our history.

The first piece of evidence Illig puts forward is the lack of actual archaeological evidence that can be reliably dated to the phantom time period. While the tie period around the Early Middle Ages has become colloquially known as the Dark Ages, it represents a fall-off from the technological and cultural high water marks of the Roman period, as the Roman Empire crumbled (or at least, as they moved their center of power from Rome to Byzantine.) To take Britain as an example, the departure of the Romans left behind a huge amount of infrastructure and architecture that could not be replicated for many hundreds of years. As the Romans pulled back throughout Europe, they left behind a cultural vacuum that other, smaller, and less dominant peoples soon stepped into. Unlike the huge ruins, artefacts, and landmarks left behind by the Romans, the peoples from this period left us with comparatively little. For Illig, this inability to use radiometrics and dendrochronological means to date items to this period is indicative of the fact that they simply did not happen. While we have come to rely on medieval writers and historians to fill us in on what happened during the period, the theory suggests that these writings were simply invented to fill in the gaps as Otto III and Sylvester II attempted to jump the calendar forwards.

The second point of evidence for the theory again turns towards the Romans in a search for proof. So dominant and influential throughout Europe, it can be easy to trace the history of the Romans across many parts of Europe even today. Whether it's their roads, their walls, or just general housing, there are few countries in Southern, Central, and Western Europe that do not possess the evidence of Roman presence in the area. But, Illig argues, the fact that some of the continent's Romanesque buildings can be dated to the tenth century demonstrates the fact that the collapse of the Roman Empire might not have been so far in the past. While it is commonly thought that the collapse of the Empire took with it the cultural and architectural advances the Romans had learned, the fact that countries were still constructing these late period Roman buildings is, the theory suggests, evidence that their demise was actually far closer to the modern day than we could have expected.

One of the more technical pieces of evidence that Illig uses involves the calendar system used during the period. The interplay between the Julian and the Gregorian calendar has caused much confusion, and it is this switch, the theory argues, that has allowed the conspiracy to alter the dates to significant effect. It begins with the Julian calendar, introduced by and named for one of the most famous Romans of all, Julius Caesar. The Julian method of dating had one notable issue, in that for every century it counted, there would be a discrepancy of one day. The Gregorian calendar, conversely, held no such issue. Introduced in 1582 AD, the people who were implementing the calendar knew the errors present in the older system and were required to back date it accordingly. With the Julian system out by a day for every century in use, this should have resulted in a discrepancy totaling thirteen days which would need to be adjusted for. However, those who introduced the calendar discovered (thanks to their mathematical and astronomical skills) that they only needed to adjust the calendar by ten days. The Julian calendar ended on the 4th of October, 1582, and the new Gregorian calendar began on the 15th of October, 1582. For Illig, this is enough evidence to suggest that there has been the removal of three centuries from the common history books sometime before. Those three missing days, as calculated by the best minds of the time, relate to the three missing centuries that were removed by the conspiracy.

Central to Illig's argument, however, is the famed figure of Charlemagne. As a key figure in European history, he is a hero in France, Germany, and many other cultures across the continent. His story of uniting various disparate tribes and bringing them all under one rule is akin to the work of Genghis Khan or Alexander the Great. Accordingly, he is apportioned the same amount of reverence. Not only was he thought to be a great warrior and statesman, but he was also an architect, an astronomer, a philosopher, and a teacher. His range of achievements is so great that, for Illig, it seems to be unbelievable. Rather than a real man, Charlemagne is a creation of those who rewrote the history books. He was literally conjured up as a folk hero and created to fit the profile of one who would have his work revered for centuries. It is not that Charlemagne is not great enough to have existed but rather, that he is too great. No one man could have accomplished everything attributed to him, so instead it must have been that the stories were embellished, exaggerated, or simply just invented in order to fill the three centuries of history that the conspiracy was attempting to insert into the calendar.

But as well as the evidence Illig puts forward for his conspiracy, others have hit back with counter arguments. The first of these brings ancient astronomical findings into the equation. We have records from the Chinese Tang dynasty that detail their exact view of the night sky. These well-dated, government approved papers actually include references to known cosmic events such as solar eclipses and the passing of Halley's Comet. When compared against the modern calendar – the one that positions us in the twenty-first century – we discover that there is no discrepancy to be found. Instead, it perfectly aligns with what is to be expected were the phantom time period theory to be false.

Secondly, when examined closely, the archaeological evidence we have gathered and tested does show that the period known as the Early Middle Ages did, in fact, exist. Rather than simply looking at the ruins of the Roman Empire, it is possible for use to recover, examine, and date the artefacts we find from around the world. Many of these locations – such as India or China – involved cultures distant to Europe, who were working under their own volition and were unencumbered by any conspiratorial efforts to dictate changes to their calendars. When we look back through their history, there is nothing to suggest that three centuries of their past have been rapidly inserted. In many cases, these cultures used very different calendars to the Julian or Gregorian systems, so the concept of 1000 AD and its importance would be entirely lost on them.

When looking closer at the theory about the discrepancies between the calendars systems, Illig's argument begins to fall apart. First, it was never the intention of the Gregorian calendar to follow on directly from the Julian calendar's beginnings in 45 BC. Instead, it was designed to trace back its lineage and start from 325 BC, the time of the Council of Nicaea. The Council, one of the most important gatherings in the history of the western world, was the meeting at which a huge amount of the doctrine of the Catholic Church was codified. As well as coming to an agreement on which books of the Bible were to be considered official, there was also established a means of figuring out the exact date of Easter Sunday. As such, the Gregorian calendar was not missing three days (equivalent to centuries) when it replaced the Julian calendar. Rather, it was purposefully designed to use calculations that began 300 years after Illig purports. This, it seems, is the source of his missing centuries.

On the subject of Charlemagne and the idea that he may have been a fabricated historical figure, this does not tally with the information which exists in other cultures around the world. For such an important figure on the European (and world) stage, it would have been impossible for Charlemagne to operate in a vacuum. As such, we see records of his actions and deeds in the recorded histories of Britain, the Vatican, and even the Byzantine Empire. As well as this, the period which Illig suggests was invented corresponds almost directly with the time when Muhammad was beginning the expansion of Islam into parts of the world which had previously been controlled by the Romans, including parts of Portugal and Spain. During the Islamic expansion, they fought battles with other cultures, including the Tang Dynasty in China. The resulting Battle of Talas was recorded by both cultures and is known to have happened during the purported phantom time period.

While Illig's theory holds a certain brash romanticism, it is has to find definitive evidence that might hold up over time. There is no need to question the motivations he ascribes to the conspirators – Otto III and Sylvester II – as the insertion of such a large period would have placed them in power at the turn of the millennium. Depending on their individual believes, this could have been a matter of great pride and importance. Instead, the conspiracy falls down simply because it is impossible to separate the history of Europe from the rest of the world. This ethnocentric approach ultimately dooms a fascinating theory. However, should Illig be able to expand his ideas and discover real evidence of a global conspiracy to invent three centuries of history, then we could be witness to one of the most dramatic, important, and interesting revelations of our time.

The PRISM Network

Of course, the very nature of conspiracy theories makes them difficult to prove. While theories such as the phantom time hypothesis might seem strange and silly to many members of the public, the fact that the idea is being discussed demonstrates the extent to which people are willing to go in their pursuit of truth. Many conspiracies have been mocked or ridiculed in their various forms, including the suggestions that the government was monitoring all of our communications. Even though theories have existed for years regarding the government's ability to spy on your digital communications, these were frequently dismissed as whack-job theories by people who wear tin foil hats. But when a huge amount of data was leaked to the world's press, it quickly became apparent that this was one conspiracy theory that turned out to be true.

The data now known as the PRISM documents was leaked by a man named Edward Snowden. These documents implicated the United States Intelligence network, Congress, the White House, and governments from around the world. It showed that the information gathering technologies that existed were far more pervasive than almost anyone had suspected up to this point. At the cornerstone of this data collection was the intelligence agency the NSA. The National Security Agency broke new grounds in the world of surveillance. With the revelations, we learned that our emails, video chats, phone calls, internet history, and almost all of our digital information was being observed, documented, and analyzed by the American security agencies. But what exactly is PRISM?

Following the terrorist attacks on September the 11th, 2001, the way in which the United States' intelligence agencies operated was overhauled. In response to the worst attack on American soil in living memory, the NSA developed a means to peruse and collect electronic data from a number of important sources. Tech giants such as Facebook, Google, Microsoft, and others were targeted. Their respective products were mined for information, a process that had its roots in the Patriot Act passed by George W. Bush, eventually becoming the Foreign Intelligence Surveillance Act that was passed over the course of 2006 and 2007.

Put simply, the PRISM system allowed for the government to request that major tech companies share data on specific people. Apple, Yahoo, Microsoft, and Google held a wealth of information, including people's email accounts, social media profiles, phone records, and essentially every other digital communication sent during the last decade. Following the revelations of the intelligence community's abilities, the government has insisted that they only collected information that was permitted under the Foreign Intelligence Surveillance Court, a body set up to overview and approve the community's investigations.

The information that Edward Snowden leaked to the world's press included a presentation designed to show the capabilities of the PRISM system. Snowden was a contractor working for the NSA who had access to the documents, which were then handed to the Guardian and the Washington Post. In this presentation, it is revealed that the NSA is able to get "direct access" to the servers of the world's biggest technology companies, something that the companies themselves have stringently denied. While both the corporates and the intelligence agencies insist the data was only collected following the granting of a court order with regards to specific, identified targets, is seems that the PRISM system is merely a streamlined approach to speed up the collection of court-approved requests for data. The presentation does not include too many technical details about how the PRISM system works, but merely demonstrates the huge capabilities that is possesses. Working at the behest of secret agencies authorized by secret courts to use secret means to collect secret data, the program has been criticized for breaches of not just privacy, but the constitutional rights of American citizens. In all, it looks like the very essence of a conspiracy theory with has been proved devastatingly true.

The man who leaked the information to the press was just 29 years old at the time. Edward Snowden had worked variously for the NSA, the CIA, and other security firms and revealed himself to be the source of the leak in the days after the story first hit the world's media. When speaking to the Guardian in an interview, he said that he did not want to be part of a society who spied so extensively on its citizens. It seems that civic duty had compelled him to reveal the truth to the world and, in turn, make himself a target for the American legal system. The leaking of classified documents is a serious crime and one which compelled Snowden to leave the United States before he had even leaked the documents. He first found refuge in Hong Kong and worked in collusion with WikiLeaks, one of the world's premier sources for the release of classified materials. After Hong Kong, he moved to Moscow and then requested asylum in a number of embassies. He has lived in this way ever since, in a kind of legal hinterland where he hopes the long reach of the American judicial system will not be able to reach him. Similar leakers (such as Chelsea Manning) have previously been held indefinitely by the American courts while they await trial.

But PRISM was not the only part of the leaked documents that caused concern. In addition to the PRISM system, the NSA ran a number of other programs designed to gather information about people. In a broad sense, these were split into two distinct categories: upstream and downstream. The former relates to the agency's ability to lift data directly from the telecommunications cables laid beneath the world's oceans, while the latter refers to the communications information collected from American tech companies. As instructed in the leaked slides of the presentation, those working for the NSA should make use of both methods when attempting to gather information.

The data collected by the intelligence agencies can be split into two groups: content and metadata. Metadata is the name for the by-products of any communications that can reveal sensitive information. So, for example, the phone records of a person can reveal information such as who was talking, the time, and the duration of the conversation, without revealing the actual content. In terms of the PRISM program, this metadata includes information about emails, instant messaging, social media, internet phone calls, cloud storage, and almost everything else a person can do on a computer. When attempting to downplay the importance of the PRISM leaks, government officials indicated that the metadata collection conducted by the NSA does not actually contain the content of the conversations or messages. It can, however, be just as illustrative. It can reveal where you were at any given time thanks to GPS. Your internet search history can reveal what you wanted to know at any given moment. Your email logs can show who you have been talking to and can build up a network of known associates in no time at all. Thanks to the lack of speed with which the law in the United States was updated, the legal measures overseeing metadata collection were far more lax than those regarding content.

One of the court orders that was leaked as part of Snowden's big reveal was the court order asking America's biggest cell phone company, Verizon, to hand over information regarding the metadata records and phone logs of every single customer. Not only this, but the company was to continue to do so on an on-going basis. Similar moves to collect internet records and metadata were enacted under a program from the Bush era named Stellarwind. This had previously been leaked by a man named William Binney but generated far less attention that the PRISM leaks. Despite lasting a few years, it has since been replaced and upgraded, with the new programs being named ShellTrumpet and EvilOlive. Though they are more capable, they have the same purpose: gather metadata about internet users.

Now that we know about the programs that are used by agencies like the NSA to collect data, the next question is to ask how they manage to undertake such a massive task. At the time of the leaks, they relied upon two key pieces of American legislation to be permitted to carry out such investigations. The first of these was Section 702 of the FISA Amendments Act. This meant that communications could be collected using PRISM and similar systems. The second piece of legislature was Section 215 of the Patriot Act, which authorized the metadata from phone companies to be collected. However, as we saw in the leaked documents, the use of secret courts had led to a far broader interpretation of these laws than might be expected. The approval of these secret courts meant that the NSA was authorized to simply collect as much information as they pleased without the need to name specific targets.

For the analysts working at the NSA, this would begin by choosing a number of "selectors," the name given to the search terms inputted into the system. Programs like PRISM would then "task" this information and would begin to gather information from a variety of sources, including phone records, email logs, and so on. It could retrieve both content and metadata. But that is not to say that there were no restrictions placed upon the agents using the systems. One of the most important was that a person could not be specifically targeted if they were "reasonably believed" to be an American citizen, communicating on American soil. As revealed in the Washington Post, an agent had to have at least 51% certainty that the person whose information they were gathering was foreign. However, because the system was set up to "chain" information (collect data on known associates and anyone linked to the person) it was easy for innocent parties to get swept up in the data collection process. The rules then demanded that the agent must try to remove the data regarding American citizens, but even the records that were not relevant to any particular case could be held for up to half a decade (or even handed over to sister agencies such as the CIA or FBI) depending on a vague range of circumstances. These circumstances include the possibility that a crime might be, is about to be, or has been committed within reasonable doubt, or when the information might be relevant to the security of the nation. The rules suggest that, if the communication data is encrypted, then it can be retained indefinitely. As it seems, the American government (and the equivalents across the world) are able to quickly, simply, and efficiently build up a portfolio of almost any person with any kind of digital presence and retain that information indefinitely. With the press of a button, PRISM and other systems can put together an entire profile of you within minutes. Thanks to the information it has access to, these profiles are unerringly accurate.

Since the information was first revealed to the world, we have had confirmation that one of the world's most widely suspected conspiracy theories turned out to be true. This collection of metadata and content was talked about for years, even as far as encroaching on the mainstream media. The big budget box office film "Enemy of the State" starring Will Smith contained technology and shady political organizations very similar to ones that were revealed by Snowden's leak. In the time since these revelations first came to light, there has been an increased pressure on the governments of the world to pull back from the brink of the information-gathering technology they possess. President Barack Obama has been criticized for the programs and has promised to shackle their abilities.

The problem with trying to tame such organizations, however, is that they are so used to working in the dark. The very nature of the intelligence community means that it is difficult to ascertain just how much they have stopped what they are doing. To the naked eye, no activity at all can appear remarkably similar to work carried out in the utmost secrecy.

But one of the most important legacies of the PRISM leaks was the way in which we were able to confirm the conspiracy theory. Unlike the majority of theories bandied about in private conversations and internet forums, we finally had a smoking gun. It leaves us with the questions: How many more will we find?

Conclusion

As we have seen over the course of this book, the notion of a conspiracy theory can be applied to everything from the mundane to the extraordinary. The various theories take us from the edge of space to our own cell phones. But the common kernel at the center of every single theory remains an obsession with truth. In every single instance, people are not satisfied with an answer and want to peel back the curtain to discover the reality about the world around them.

In that respect, it is why it is so important that we pay attention to the leaked documents surrounding the PRISM system. Here, we have a conspiracy theory that was dismissed by many and considered to be a work of science fiction. But eventually, the truth will out. While we may never come across the real answers behind the assassination of John F. Kennedy or the truth behind the moon landing, we can live in hope that one piece of evidence might rise to the surface and clarify and enlighten the world around us.

If you are still interested in the idea of conspiracy theories, there is a further reading list at the end of this book. If you have read through the various chapters, the one thing you might want to take away is the importance of casting a critical eye on the world around you. Even when everything seems to be simple, it can help to take an alternative appraisal of everything you think you know.

Further Reading

Aaronovitch, D. (2010). *Voodoo histories*. London: Vintage.

Burnett, T. (2005). *Conspiracy encyclopedia*. New York: Chamberlain Bros.

King, J. (2010). *Conspiracy theories*. Chichester: Summersdale.

King, J. (n.d.). *Conspiracy theories*.

Lewis, J. (2009). *The Mammoth Book of Cover-Ups*. London: Constable & Robinson.

Marrs, J. (2010). *The trillion-dollar conspiracy*. New York: William Morrow.

McConnachie, J. and Tudge, R. (2013). *The rough guide to conspiracy theories*. London: Rough Guides.

Munroe, R. (2015). *What if?*. [S.l.]: John Murray Publishers Lt.

Shircore, I. (2012). *Conspiracy!*. London, England: AdLib.

Smith, D. (n.d.). *100 things they don't want you to know*. Quercus Publishing Plc.

Thomas, A. (2013). *Conspiracies*. London: Watkins Publishing.

Excerpt from Conrad Bauer's book The Knights Templar: The Hidden History of the Knights Templar: The Church's Oldest Conspiracy

The Knights Templar existed officially for less than 200 years. Founded to protect pilgrims who were traveling through the Holy Lands, their rise to power was sudden. They became some of the most feared warriors in the region, they had a mandate from God, they controlled perhaps the world's first real banking system, and they waged war against anyone who tried to wrestle Christianity's holiest grounds from the control of the Catholic Church. Within their short lifespan, they quickly became one of the most powerful societies in Europe, if not the world.

But, just as they rose to power with relative speed, they fell from grace just as fast. Forged in the crucible of Middle Eastern conflict, their power was soon resented and feared. Before they could become even more powerful, the greatest nations in Europe and the Church turned on them. The once powerful Templars were hunted, caught, tortured, and eventually burned at the stake. According to their prosecutors, they were a devil-worshipping secret society who spat on the cross and plotted against the Pope. They were officially disbanded and their members treated with extreme contempt and prejudice.

Or so goes the official story. In this book, we will not only look into the official history of the Knights Templar, but will examine the various ways their influence and ideas have tunnelled their way into the modern world. A group this powerful does not vanish overnight. Instead, their history has been linked to the Freemasons, to vicious curses, to the butchery of the Crusades, and even to Christian relics such as the Holy Grail. For many people, the Templars did not vanish and they did not relinquish their tight grip on the power structures of medieval Europe. Instead, they went underground. Read on to discover the dark and twisted secret history of the Knights Templar.

The Savagery of the First Crusade

It is important to understand the context in which the Knights Templar were founded. Their formation was not as simple as a group of knights agreeing to gather together under one banner. Instead, their order was forged in the midst of the violence, conflict, and religious turmoil that was the medieval Holy Land. Much like our world today, the Near East of the turn of the first century was not a calm place. For centuries, it had been the area from which many of the world's major religions had been formed. The three huge Abrahamic religions – Judaism, Christianity, and Islam – were all born in the same area. Indeed, they share many of the same principles, historical figures, and even religious texts. With all three religions deriving from the same geographical location, the fight for supremacy in the region led to constant conflict.

To Western readers, this conflict is most familiar through the Crusades. From the Christian perspective, the Crusades were a series of military campaigns waged in the Near East and divinely sanctioned by the Catholic Church. At the time, Islam controlled much of the region and Christian pilgrims were struggling to find safe passage to the holy sites they wished to visit. Christianity was facing a major schism, as the collapse of the Roman Empire had led to divisions forming between the Western head of the Church in the Vatican in Rome and his Eastern equivalent in Byzantine (the city later known as Constantinople and eventually Istanbul.) According to historian Paul Everett Pierson, Pope Urban II not only saw the first campaign as a chance to protect Christians in the Holy Land, but as a chance to reunite the disparate branches of the Church back under his control.

Protection for Pilgrims

The first Crusade was prompted by a letter sent from the Byzantine Emperor Alexios I in 1095. Alexios begged the Pope for assistance, knowing that the head of the Church might be able to rally an army in order to protect the citizens from around the world who were attempting to make the journey to holy sites in cities such as Jerusalem as these citizens were often finding themselves in trouble. Though the Muslim rulers in Palestine and throughout the Holy Land nominally allowed for Catholic pilgrims to journey through their lands without an issue, this was not always the reality. The crimes supposedly committed by the Muslim rulers in the Holy Land were violent, vicious, and offensive to Christian sensibilities. These included suggestions that the Turks who controlled the area had ravaged the churches belonging to Christians in the region, that they had captured the city of Christ (Jerusalem) and had blasphemed against it by selling the Christian institutions (government offices, shops, merchants, tax offices, etc.) into abominable slavery, and that they had been harassing, bullying, and even committing acts of violence against the good Christians who simply wished to journey to the land of their savior.

As with many proclamations calling for violence and war, however, these claims were likely exaggerated. Emperor Alexios was himself facing a difficult reign, his Byzantine Empire having to disband their standing army following economic worries and the inflation of their currency. He needed help projecting power in the region, so turned to the place where his empire had traditionally been associated: Rome. He begged the Pope for assistance, for the military liberation of the region, and for help in turning back the wave of Muslim rule imposed by the conquering Turks.

In November of 1095, the Catholic Church held a conference to determine whether or not to assist Alexios. The Council of Clermont is documented in a number of different contemporary texts, by a number of writers who may have been present at the Council. The accounts do not tell the same story. Robert the Monk – who was present – suggests that Pope Urban decreed that it was God's will to intervene in the region. In return, Robert writes, the Pope promised absolution (forgiveness for mortal sins) to the men who would become crusaders. Other sources have suggested that the Pope instead offered an indulgence (an award that would reduce the punishment for any sins committed.) However, all of our accounts remember that the Pope focused more on the conquest of the Holy Lands, rather than providing assistance to the Byzantine Empire. It was agreed that the mission would be put into motion on the 15th of August, a date important in the Catholic Church. Led by Adhemar of Le Puy, the first Crusade would set out on the same day as the Assumption of Mary.

Preparing for the Crusade

In a pre-Reformation Europe, the Catholic Church held a monopoly over religion. All Christian doctrine and its interpretation flowed through the corridors of Vatican City. While only a small district within the once-powerful city of Rome, the Vatican's power was on a similar level to that of France, Britain, and the other major countries. At the time, however, the Church had no standing army. If they were to launch a Crusade – a military campaign – then they would need soldiers. Not only would they need troops to fight, they would need men to lead. As such, Pope Urban issued his decree to the countries around Europe and requested that they send men of high and low birth to fight on behalf of the church. As well as the soldiers, a preacher named Peter the Hermit gathered together a group of 20,000 pilgrims and began the journey to the Holy Land.

But they did not travel far before they became embroiled in controversy and religious warfare. In 1096, as the 20,000 pilgrims passed through the Rhineland in Germany, they came across the cities of Worms, Speyer, Cologne, and Mainz. At the time, these cities had large Jewish communities. Such was the religious fervor of those embarking upon the First Crusade, that these Jewish communities presented an easy target for the mob's pent up wrath. As well as this, it was their first chance to practice their violence on a large scale. Bands of both knights and peasants who were traveling with the group became increasingly violent as they encountered Jewish communities. This violence included attempts at forced conversion, beatings, torture, and execution.

Perhaps the most violent of these early Crusader armies was the one lead by Count Emicho. Under his authority, a group of 10,000 Crusaders – both nobility and peasants – began to slaughter Jewish communities in large numbers. Though many of the local clergy objected – as did the Catholic Church itself – there was little that could be done to stop the marauding bands of Crusaders. Communities of 800, 900, and even 1,000 were killed. Sources tell of one Jewish man who, after being forcibly converted to Christianity, was so overcome with the guilt of his actions that his killed his entire family and himself. One woman, hoping to escape the cruel violence of the Crusaders, killed her entire family before they could be subjected to the whims of the massed ranks. For historian David Nirenberg, the events of late 1096 planted the seeds of violent anti-Semitism which would eventually grow into the horrific slaughter of the Holocaust. The Rhineland massacres – as they came to be known – were an early indication of the kind of religious warfare promised by the Crusades.

Arriving in the Holy Land

The main army of the Crusaders was composed of French and Norman knights, backed up by soldiers from across Europe. They fought under the banner of the Church, with up to 100,000 men journeying to Byzantine to wage their war. Because they fought for a religious cause, the Church was able to offer them spiritual rewards. The importance of promises such as indulgences or absolution meant that not only would crimes committed during the Crusades be forgiven, but that sins already committed at home were less likely to deny the perpetrator entrance into the kingdom of heaven. For those who fervently believed in the Christian faith, this was a cause they could get behind.

Once the forces had gathered in modern-day Istanbul, the Crusade could begin in earnest. It was not a short campaign, lasting for many years. One of the first major conflicts came when the Crusaders tried to take the city of Antioch and laid siege to the city. Though the residents lasted almost a year behind the walls, they eventually fell to the Crusaders. Once inside, the Christians offered no quarter in their treatment of the Muslim population. They slaughtered them, soldiers and civilians both. The sacking of the city was so complete that a Muslim army was able to creep up on the Crusaders and lay siege to the city themselves. The Crusaders rallied their troops within Antioch and went out to meet the army being led by Muslim commander Kerbogha. They triumphed and held on to the strategically important city.

The Battle for Jerusalem

From Antioch, the majority of the Crusader army marched south. Their goal – as it had been from the start – was to take the city in the name of Christianity. At the time, it was under Islamic control, but the city's population of Jews were able to live and practice their religion in relative peace. Even visiting Christian pilgrims were permitted to visit the holy sites and pray. This was not enough. Jerusalem was to be under Christian rule and the Crusaders would fight tooth and nail to wrest the city from their enemy's grasp.

Both the Muslims and Jews within Jerusalem fought long and hard against the Crusaders. But they would not hold out forever. On the 15th of July, 1099, the Christians took control of the city. What followed was a massacre. Much like at Antioch, the Crusaders pillaged the city. Anyone found to be a Muslim or a Jew was killed. Civilians were slaughtered en masse. The buildings that had been erected by Islamic architects were torn down, from mosques to other civil institutions. For one Crusader, Raymond D'Aguilers, the massacre was vindicated. He wrote a book titled 'Historia Francorum qui ceperunt Iherusalem,' in which he describes the Christians' entry into the city. His description of the Temple Mount suggests that the Crusaders' butchery was so great that blood rose to the knees of the men as they rode their horses.

Another source – Fulcher of Chartres – tells of 10,000 citizens being slaughtered, including women and children. Others report that the stench of the dead bodies was so great that they had to be carried beyond the city walls and left to rot outside. The funeral pyres, we are told, were so big they resembled pyramids. Only God alone could know the true number of men, women, and children killed that day.

Following the capture of Jerusalem, the Crusaders had control of four major cities in the Holy Land. These were Antioch, Tripoli, Edessa, and — the jewel in the crown —

Jerusalem. For historians such as Riley Smith, however, the result of the First Crusade was not simply the territory now under Christian control, but the 'wave of pious, Catholic fury' which had been unleashed. The various massacres stretching from Germany to Jerusalem were indicative of the extent to which the Catholic Church's armies were able to use violence to achieve their goals.

After this campaign of violence, it seemed as though the Church had been at least partially successful. The Crusade had provided a banner under which Christians could unite and had exhibited the military power that the Church was able to project. For Christian pilgrims, passage to the Holy Land was now much safer. With Tripoli and Antioch both lying close to the Mediterranean Sea, the journey to Jerusalem could be conducted along Christian-held routes. But while protection for these pilgrims had initially been a goal, it had been supplanted in the name of control. Passage for Christians was not enough; now, they had to hold on to the Holy Lands.

Following a period of fearsome, church-backed violence, this was the world into which the Knights Templar would emerge. Already tainted by the violent butchery of the

First Crusade, the blood of the massacres would linger over their formation and dictate their doctrine from their very first moments.

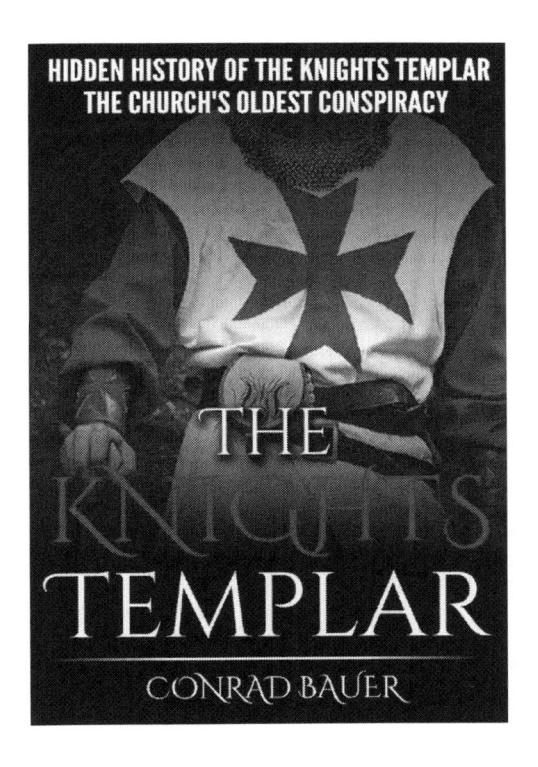

About the author

Conrad Bauer is passionate about everything paranormal, unexplained, mysterious, and terrifying. It comes from his childhood and the famous stories his grandfather used to tell the family during summer vacation camping trips. He vividly remembers his grandfather sitting around the fire with new stories to tell everyone who would gather around and listen. His favorites were about the paranormal, including ghost stories, haunted houses, strange places, and paranormal occurrences.

Bauer is an adventurous traveller who has gone to many places in search of the unexplained and paranormal. He has been researching the paranormal and what scares people for more than four decades. He also loves to dig into period of history that are still full of mysteries, being an avid reader of the mystic secret societies that have mark history and remain fascinating and legendary throughout the times. He has accumulated a solid expertise and knowledge that he now shares through his books with his readers and followers.

Conrad, now retired, lives in the countryside in Ireland with his wife and two dogs.

More Books from Conrad Bauer

Printed in Great Britain
by Amazon